OLD TESTAMENT CHARACTERS

MOSES

BY JOHN HOLDSWORTH

INTRODUCTION

The story of the people of Israel, the descendants of the family of Jacob, is part of the Old Testament. God gave Jacob the name Israel and so his family came to be known as the "children of Israel" or "the Israelites". (In this book and in the Bible passages quoted they are also called "Israelites" and "Hebrews".) God promised Jacob that one day his family would have many descendants and that they would live in a land of their own. This was the same promise he had made to Jacob's grandfather, Abraham.

One of Jacob's sons, Joseph, was brought to Egypt as a slave but became an important advisor to the king. Since Joseph now had a position of great authority, his father Jacob, and all the family came to live with him in Egypt (see Genesis 37-50). Several years later Joseph died, but his family stayed in Egypt. Generations later the population of Israelites in Egypt had grown so much that the Egyptians themselves began to feel threatened by having so many foreigners in their country, and they began to force them into slavery. But the Israelites continued to grow in numbers. Eventually a king came to power who took still more drastic action. He commanded that every new-born Hebrew boy must be thrown into the Nile. It was at this time, more than 1200 years before the birth of Jesus, that Moses was born.

SESSION ONE

The abandoned baby

The story of Moses is told in the book of Exodus. Exodus means "journey out" and most of the book is about the journey made by the Israelites out of Egypt to the land promised to them by God. Moses played an important part in this, as we shall see, so Exodus opens with the story of his birth.

[1] During this time a man from the tribe of Levi married a woman of his own tribe, [2] and she bore him a son. When she saw what a fine baby he was, she hid him for three months. [3] But when she could not hide him any longer, she took a basket made of reeds and covered it with tar to make it watertight. She put the baby in it and then placed it in the tall grass at the edge of the river. [4] The baby's sister stood some distance away to see what would happen to him.

[5] The king's daughter came down to the river to bathe, while her servants walked along the bank. Suddenly she noticed the basket in the tall grass and sent a slave-girl to get it. [6] The princess opened it and saw a baby boy. He was crying, and she felt sorry for him. "This is one of the Hebrew babies," she said.

[7] Then his sister asked her, "Shall I go and call a Hebrew woman to act as a wet-nurse?"

[8] "Please do," she answered. So the girl went and brought the baby's own mother. [9] The princess told the woman, "Take this baby and nurse him for me, and I will pay you." So she took the baby and nursed him. [10] Later, when the child was old enough, she took him to the king's daughter, who adopted him as her own son. She said to herself, "I pulled him out of the water, and so I name him Moses". *Exodus 2.1-10*

To talk about

- This is what newspaper editors would call a good "human interest" story. Suppose you were a reporter sent out to write the story up: who would you interview, and what would you ask them? As a group, take turns at acting out the interviews. Would any of these headlines fit your story?
  - DESPAIRING MOTHER DUMPS BABY
  - HOME FOUND FOR HIDDEN CHILD
  - THE ONE THAT GOT AWAY
  - Can you suggest any other possible headlines?

- The writer goes into great detail about what happened when Moses was born. Do you think this is because:
  - it is such an exciting story?
  - it shows how God can overcome difficulties?
  - it explains how Moses has kind of dual nationality - born a Hebrew but brought up as an Egyptian?
  - Can you think of any other reasons?

New Testament link

When people write life stories they tend to concentrate on the parts they think are really important. For instance, though we know something about Moses as a baby, we know nothing about his childhood in the Egyptian palace.

In fact, the way a story is written tells us a lot about the purpose of the author.

Take a look at Matthew 2.1-15 to learn about some of the events which took place at the time when Jesus was born . . .

¹ Jesus was born in the town of Bethlehem in Judaea, during the time when Herod was king. Soon afterwards, some men who studied the stars came from the east to Jerusalem ² and asked, "Where is the baby born to be the king of the Jews? We saw his star when it came up in the east, and we have come to worship him."

³ When King Herod heard about this, he was very upset, and so was everyone else in Jerusalem. ⁴ He called together all the chief priests and the teachers of the Law and asked them, "Where will the Messiah be born?"

⁵ "In the town of Bethlehem in Judaea," they answered. "For this is what the prophet wrote:

⁶ 'Bethlehem in the land of Judah,
    you are by no means the least of the leading
      cities of Judah;
  for from you will come a leader
  who will guide my people Israel.' "

⁷ So Herod called the visitors from the east to a secret meeting and found out from them the exact time the star had appeared. ⁸ Then he sent them to Bethlehem with these instructions: "Go and make a careful search for the child, and when you find him, let me know, so that I too may go and worship him."

⁹⁻¹⁰ And so they left, and on their way they saw the same star they had seen in the east. When they saw it, how happy they were, what joy was theirs! It went ahead of them until it stopped over the place where the child was. ¹¹ They went into the house, and when they saw the child with his mother Mary, they knelt down and worshipped him. They brought out their gifts of gold, frankincense, and myrrh, and presented them to him.

¹² Then they returned to their country by another road, since God had warned them in a dream not to go back to Herod.

¹³ After they had left, an angel of the Lord appeared in a dream to Joseph and said, "Herod will be looking for the child in order to kill him. So get up, take the child and his mother and escape to Egypt, and stay there until I tell you to leave."

¹⁴ Joseph got up, took the child and his mother, and left during the night for Egypt, ¹⁵ where he stayed until Herod died. This was done to make what the Lord had said through the prophet come true, "I called my Son out of Egypt."

• What do these events tell us about Moses and Jesus?

Moses escapes to Midian

¹¹ When Moses had grown up, he went out to visit his people, the Hebrews, and he saw how they were forced to do hard labour. He even saw an Egyptian kill a Hebrew, one of Moses' own people. ¹² Moses looked all round, and when he saw that no one was watching, he killed the Egyptian and hid his body in the sand. ¹³ The next day he went back and saw two Hebrew men fighting. He said to the one who was in the wrong, "Why are you beating up a fellow-Hebrew?"

¹⁴ The man answered, "Who made you our ruler and judge? Are you going to kill me just as you killed that Egyptian?" Then Moses was afraid and said to himself, "People have found out what I have done." ¹⁵ When the king heard about what had happened, he tried to have Moses killed, but Moses fled and went to live in the land of Midian.
Exodus 2.11-15

- Look at these headlines. Which would you choose for the newspaper account of this incident?
  - TRAITOR!
    "THIS IS HOW HE REPAYS OUR KINDNESS," SAYS PRINCESS

  - RACIAL KILLING?
    "I THINK HE WAS TRYING TO PROVE SOMETHING," SAYS SLAVE-DRIVER

  - ROUGH JUSTICE!
    SLAVE-DRIVERS WARNED TO CONTROL ABUSES. "THIS COULD HAVE BEEN AVOIDED," SAYS ISRAELITE BOSS

- Moses kills the Egyptian because he killed a Hebrew slave. What happens as a result?
- Does this story tell us anything about violence as a means to an end?

Then and now

- Are there issues today that you feel so strongly about you are tempted to take matters into your own hands, as Moses did? Share these in pairs.

Life in Midian

Moses is now an exile in the land of Midian, far from his native country. It is interesting that the people Moses meets think he is an Egyptian.

[16] One day, when Moses was sitting by a well, seven daughters of Jethro, the priest of Midian, came to draw water and fill the troughs for their father's sheep and goats. [17] But some shepherds drove Jethro's daughters away. Then Moses went to their rescue and

watered their animals for them. [18] When they returned
to their father, he asked, "Why have you come back so
early today?"

[19] "An Egyptian rescued us from the shepherds," they
answered, "and he even drew water for us and
watered our animals."

[20] "Where is he?" he asked his daughters. "Why did
you leave the man out there? Go and invite him to
eat with us."

[21] So Moses agreed to live there, and Jethro gave
him his daughter Zipporah in marriage, [22] who bore
him a son.   *Exodus 2.16-22*

Moses has settled down with Jethro's family and lives
in Midian for many years. Now the scene switches
back to Egypt . . .

[23] Years later the king of Egypt died, but the Israelites
were still groaning under their slavery and cried out
for help. Their cry went up to God, [24] who heard their
groaning and remembered his covenant with
Abraham, Isaac, and Jacob.   *Exodus 2.23-24*

The covenant God had made with Abraham, Isaac and
Jacob was his promise that their descendants, the
Israelites, would live in a land of their own. It wasn't
a one-sided contract: the Israelites also made a
promise, which was "You will be our God".

So far the story has had a lot to say about power. The
Israelites seem powerless, and they need help. Who
will be powerful enough to help them? What will the
powerful king of Egypt do? How will God show his
power? Through the frightened exile, Moses? These
are the issues which we will look at in the next
session.

SESSION TWO

The burning bush

At the end of our last session, Moses was living with his father-in-law, Jethro, in the Land of Midian. As we pick up the story, something strange happens . . .

¹ One day while Moses was taking care of the sheep and goats of his father-in-law Jethro, the priest of Midian, he led the flock across the desert and came to Sinai, the holy mountain. ² There the angel of the LORD appeared to him as a flame coming from the middle of a bush. Moses saw that the bush was on fire but that it was not burning up. ³ "This is strange," he thought. "Why isn't the bush burning up? I will go closer and see."

⁴ When the LORD saw that Moses was coming closer, he called to him from the middle of the bush and said, "Moses! Moses!"

He answered, "Yes, here I am."

⁵ God said, "Do not come any closer. Take off your sandals, because you are standing on holy ground. ⁶ I am the God of your ancestors, the God of Abraham, Isaac, and Jacob." So Moses covered his face, because he was afraid to look at God.   *Exodus 3.1-6*

God asks Moses to take off his sandals. This is a mark of respect because Moses is in God's presence.

To talk about

- Look at this list of things that people sometimes do when they pray. Which do you think are useful? Can you add to the list?

- Close eyes
- Put hands together
- Face in a particular direction
- Kneel down
- Cover the head
- Wear special clothes

- Why do you think these things are important? Do they:
  - make you feel that you are small and God is great?
  - make you feel that you are less perfect than God?
  - help you concentrate?
  - make you feel the occasion is special?
  - make you feel anything else?

God cares for his people

Notice that God introduces himself to Moses as the God of Abraham, Isaac and Jacob. That is, he is the God who looked after the Israelites for many years and he continues to care for them now.

- God calls Moses to lead the people of Israel out of slavery in Egypt. Is Moses the obvious choice for this job? Perhaps his inside knowledge of the Egyptian court will help him, but is he a natural leader?
- Is it always possible to tell why God chooses someone for a particular task?

New Testament link

- In response to God's call Moses says "I am nobody". Would the story have been different if he had said "Yes, I'll go. You couldn't have a better man for the job"?

Read the following passage from a letter written by the apostle Paul to the Christians at Corinth...

[21] For God in his wisdom made it impossible for people to know him by means of their own wisdom. Instead, by means of the so-called "foolish" message we preach, God decided to save those who believe. [22] Jews want miracles for proof, and Greeks look for wisdom. [23] As for us, we proclaim the crucified Christ, a message that is offensive to the Jews and nonsense to the Gentiles; [24] but for those whom God has called, both Jews and Gentiles, this message is Christ, who is the power of God and the wisdom of God. [25] For what seems to be God's foolishness is wiser than human wisdom, and what seems to be God's weakness is stronger than human strength. *1 Corinthians 1.21-25*

• What does this say about the people God calls?

Sent in God's name

In the Old Testament, names are very important. Look at the passage in which Moses learns God's name . . .

[13] But Moses replied, "When I go to the Israelites and say to them, 'The God of your ancestors sent me to you,' they will ask me, 'What is his name?' So what can I tell them?"

[14] God said, "I am who I am. This is what you must say to them: 'The one who is called I AM has sent me to you.' [15] Tell the Israelites that I, the LORD, the God of their ancestors, the God of Abraham, Isaac, and Jacob, have sent you to them. This is my name for ever; this is what all future generations are to call me. [16] Go and gather the leaders of Israel together and tell them that I, the LORD, the God of their ancestors, the God of Abraham, Isaac, and Jacob, appeared to you. Tell them that I have come to them and have seen

what the Egyptians are doing to them. [17] I have
decided that I will bring them out of Egypt, where
they are being treated cruelly, and will take them to a
rich and fertile land - the land of the Canaanites, the
Hittites, the Amorites, the Perizzites, the Hivites, and
the Jebusites.

[18] "My people will listen to what you say to them.
Then you must go with the leaders of Israel to the
king of Egypt and say to him, 'The LORD, the God of
the Hebrews, has revealed himself to us. Now allow us
to travel for three days into the desert to offer
sacrifices to the LORD, our God.' [19] I know that the
king of Egypt will not let you go unless he is forced to
do so. [20] But I will use my power and will punish
Egypt by doing terrifying things there. After that he
will let you go.   *Exodus 3.13-20*

• Moses has to persuade his own people and the
  Egyptian king that God has sent him to them. If
  you were Moses' Public Relations Officer, how
  would you help him to do this? Take turns in trying
  to convince other members of the group. Look back
  at the passage to see what God says Moses should
  do.

For the Israelites a name described its owner. Moses
was pulled out of the water as a baby and so he was
given a name which sounds like the Hebrew word
meaning "to pull out". Your name told others what
kind of person you were. The Israelites knew about
the covenant God made with their ancestors, but by
telling Moses his name, God revealed more of his
identity and Moses came to know God in a special
way.

In the original Hebrew, God's name is written YHWH
which means "I am who I am" or "I will be who I will
be". In English it is usually written Yahweh.

- Many different titles are used to describe God in the Bible, such as Judge, Lord, King, Father. Can you think of others?
- Which title best suits the way you picture God? Can you explain why?

Then and now

God has given Moses a difficult task and Moses doesn't feel he's the right person for the job. Yet God has promised him help and success in the end.

- Has there ever been a time when you have faced a difficult situation and felt as Moses did? Share any thoughts in pairs.

SESSION THREE

The reluctant messenger

In the last session we saw how God called Moses to do a job for him. Moses was not very confident about his ability to do it. As we pick up the story again, we see he's still worried . . .

¹ Then Moses answered the LORD, "But suppose the Israelites do not believe me and will not listen to what I say. What shall I do if they say that you did not appear to me?"

² So the LORD asked him, "What are you holding?"

"A stick," he answered.

³ The LORD said, "Throw it on the ground." When Moses threw it down, it turned into a snake, and he ran away from it. ⁴ Then the LORD said to Moses, "Bend down and pick it up by the tail." So Moses bent down and caught it, and it became a stick again. ⁵ The LORD said, "Do this to prove to the Israelites that the LORD, the God of their ancestors, the God of Abraham, Isaac, and Jacob, has appeared to you."

⁶ The LORD spoke to Moses again, "Put your hand inside your robe." Moses obeyed; and when he took his hand out, it was diseased, covered with white spots, like snow. ⁷ Then the LORD said, "Put your hand inside your robe again." He did so, and when he took it out this time, it was healthy, just like the rest of his body. ⁸ The LORD said, "If they will not believe you or be convinced by the first miracle, then this one will convince them. ⁹ If in spite of these two miracles they still will not believe you, and if they refuse to listen to what you say, take some water from the Nile and pour it on the ground. The water will turn into blood."

[10] But Moses said, "No, LORD, don't send me. I have never been a good speaker, and I haven't become one since you began to speak to me. I am a poor speaker, slow and hesitant."

[11] The LORD said to him, "Who gives man his mouth? Who makes him deaf or dumb? Who gives him sight or makes him blind? It is I, the LORD. [12] Now, go! I will help you to speak, and I will tell you what to say."

[13] But Moses answered, "No, Lord, please send someone else."

[14] At this the LORD became angry with Moses and said, "What about your brother Aaron, the Levite? I know that he can speak well. In fact, he is now coming to meet you and will be glad to see you. [15] You can speak to him and tell him what to say. I will help both of you to speak, and I will tell you both what to do. [16] He will be your spokesman and speak to the people for you. Then you will be like God, telling him what to say. [17] Take this stick with you; for with it you will perform miracles." *Exodus 4.1-17*

It seems Moses hasn't got the message yet that God can help him carry off an extraordinary mission. He's still worried because he's not a good speaker.

To talk about

As we'll read later on, Moses and Aaron go on to work as a team and may become great leaders together. The secret of their successful partnership lies in their different gifts. Moses listens to God; Aaron speaks to the people. In this way each makes up for what the other lacks.

- Make a list of leaders in your own church community. What qualities and skills do they have which help them to be effective leaders?

- Are there differences between churches led by one person and churches with a team of leaders? Discuss the advantages and disadvanges of each.

Back to Egypt

At God's command, Moses returns to the Israelites in Egypt . . .

¹⁸ Then Moses went back to Jethro, his father-in-law, and said to him, "Please let me go back to my relatives in Egypt to see if they are still alive." Jethro agreed and said good-bye to him.

¹⁹ While Moses was still in Midian, the LORD said to him, "Go back to Egypt, for all those who wanted to kill you are dead." ²⁰ So Moses took his wife and his sons, put them on a donkey, and set out with them for Egypt, carrying the stick that God had told him to take.

²⁷ Meanwhile the LORD had said to Aaron, "Go into the desert to meet Moses." So he went to meet him at the holy mountain; and when he met him, he kissed him. ²⁸ Then Moses told Aaron everything that the LORD had said when he told him to return to Egypt; he also told him about the miracles which the LORD had ordered him to perform. ²⁹ So Moses and Aaron went to Egpyt and gathered all the Israelite leaders together. ³⁰ Aaron told them everything that the LORD had said to Moses, and then Moses performed all the miracles in front of the people. ³¹ They believed, and when they heard that the LORD had come to them and had seen how they were being treated cruelly, they bowed down and worshipped.   *Exodus 4.18-20, 27-31*

- Imagine being among the Israelites at that time. What do you think the main theme of your worship would be? How about one of these?

- Celebrating God's love for his chosen people
- Thanks to God for his offer of help

- Can you think of an approriate hymn or prayer that would be familiar today?

Signs of God's power at work

For people who believe in God, miracles are signs of God's power. Moses and Aaron perform miracles in front of the people and later in front of the king, they get completely different reactions. The Israelites recognize that Moses is sent by God because of the miracles he performs. However, the king has no faith in Moses' God and refuses to listen. In fact, he thinks the miracles are just magic.

- Are all miracles events which cannot be explained?

New Testament Link

Jesus was not the only miracle-worker in his day but the gospel-writers were convinced that the power of God was at work in him in a special way.

Look at Matthew 11.2-6 . . .

> [2] When John the Baptist heard in prison about the things that Christ was doing, he sent some of his disciples to him. [3] "Tell us," they asked Jesus, "are you the one John said was going to come, or should we expect someone else?"
>
> [4] Jesus answered, "Go back and tell John what you are hearing and seeing: [5] the blind can see, the lame can walk, those who suffer from dreaded skin-diseases are made clean, the deaf hear, the dead are brought back to life, and the Good News is preached to the

poor. [6] How happy are those who have no doubts about
me!"

All the gospel-writers saw Jesus' miracles as signs
that he is the Messiah. God's chosen one.

- When you say something is a miracle, what do you
  mean?
- Do you know anyone who believes they have seen a
  miracle?
- What do miracles tell you about God?

Then and Now

When Moses needed help, God gave him the power to
work the miracles and a partner, Aaron.

- Has God ever given you help when you really
  needed it? How did it happen?

SESSION FOUR

Let my people go . . .

At the end of the last session, Moses and Aaron were about to see the king of Egypt. Now read about their first meeting with him . . .

> [1] Then Moses and Aaron went to the king of Egypt and said, "The LORD, the God of Israel, says, 'Let my people go, so that they can hold a festival in the desert to honour me.'"
>
> [2] "Who is the LORD?" the king demanded. "Why should I listen to him and let Israel go? I do not know the LORD; and I will not let Israel go."
>
> [3] Moses and Aaron replied, "The God of the Hebrews has revealed himself to us. Allow us to travel for three days into the desert to offer sacrifices to the LORD our God. If we don't do so, he will kill us with disease or by war."
>
> [4] The king said to Moses and Aaron, "What do you mean by making the people neglect their work? Get those slaves back to work! [5] You people have become more numerous than the Egyptians. And now you want to stop working!"   *Exodus 5.1-5*

Moses and Aaron call God by the name which he revealed to Moses at the burning bush: YHWH. (In most English translations of the Bible, LORD is used to represent YHWH.)

This first meeting with the king is only the beginning of lengthy negotiations. To start with, Moses and Aaron just ask for a short holiday so that the Israelites can worship their God. However, the king responds by being even more harsh on the people . . .

17

⁶ That same day the king commanded the Eyptian slave-drivers and the Israelite foremen: ⁷ "Stop giving the people straw for making bricks. Make them go and find it for themselves. ⁸ But still require them to make the same number of bricks as before, not one brick less. They haven't enough work to do, and that is why they keep asking me to let them go and offer sacrifices to their God! ⁹ Make these men work harder and keep them busy, so that they won't have time to listen to a pack of lies."   *Exodus 5.6-9*

Because the people can't meet the king's new demand they are punished. It is hardly surprising that they blame Moses and Aaron for their troubles. So Moses complains to God . . .

²² Then Moses turned to the LORD again and said, "Lord, why do you ill-treat your people? Why did you send me here? ²³ Ever since I went to the king to speak for you, he has treated them cruelly. And you have done nothing to help them!"

¹ Then the LORD said to Moses, "Now you are going to see what I will do to the king. I will force him to let my people go. In fact, I will force him to drive them out of his land."   *Exodus 5.22-6.1*

To Talk about

Imagine yourself as the Industrial Correspondent of Egyptian TV News. You are standing outside the king's palace in front of the cameras with a mike in your hand. You begin your report something like this:

"A new meeting between negotiating team Moses and Aaron and the king is expected any time. A group of foremen saw the king earlier but reported no change. These men are angry about details of the new productivity scheme which came into effect when demands for holidays were turned down . . ."

- In the group, try acting out interviews with the king, Moses and Aaron, and the foremen.
- What do you think is important if you are to put up a convincing argument in negotiations:
  - to believe that you are have a valid case and are in the right?
  - to have power on your side?
  - to keep your side united behind you and be sure that the opposition don't divide you?

Disasters strike Egypt

The king has shown his power - now Moses and Aaron show God's power. Disasters strike Egypt. They are all possible natural occurrences but the king accepts that they are the actions of God. However, he does not give in easily.

This section of the book of Exodus is sometimes known as the "Ten Plagues". First the country is covered with frogs. Swarms of gnats come, followed by swarms of flies. Other disasters include outbreaks of boils and sores, and the death of the Egyptians' animals. Here is an example . . .

[16] The LORD said to Moses, "Tell Aaron to strike the ground with his stick, and all over the land of Egypt the dust will change into gnats." [17] So Aaron struck the ground with his stick, and all the dust in Egypt was turned into gnats, which covered the people and the animals. [18] The magicians tried to use their magic to make gnats appear, but they failed. There were gnats everywhere, [19] and the magicians said to the king, "God has done this!" But the king was stubborn and, just as the LORD had said, the king would not listen to Moses and Aaron. *Exodus 8.16-19*

- On your own, look at the list below. Which of the following do you think God really wants? Give each possibility a mark from 0 (not likely) to 5 (most likely):
  - freedom for the people?
  - the king to know that the earth belongs to the Lord?
  - the Egyptians to know that they have sinned against God?
  - the Egyptians to be bitten by gnats?
  - freedom of worship for the people of Israel?

- Look at the scores you have given. What picture of God do they suggest? Compare your scores with the rest of the group.

The worst disaster

After nine "plagues", the king still refuses to let the Israelites go. But the final disaster is the most terrible of all.

> [4] Moses then said to the king, "The LORD says, 'At about midnight I will go through Egypt, [5] and every first-born son in Egypt will die, from the king's son, who is heir to the throne, to the son of the slave-woman, who grinds corn. The first-born of all the cattle will die also. [6] There will be loud crying all over Egypt, such as there has never been before or ever will be again. [7] But not even a dog will bark at the Israelites or their animals. Then you will know that I, the LORD, make a distinction between the Egyptians and the Israelites.'" *Exodus 11.4-7*

This proves to be the final straw for the king, and the people escape. The events surrounding this final disaster, the death of the Egyptians' first-born sons, continue to be remembered today in a special festival celebrated by Jews called the Passover.

Then and now

- Is there anything about the activity of God in this part of the story that you find disturbing? Share this with the other members of the group Remember that the story is being told from the Israelite point of view.
- Does the story have anything to say to Christians today who are facing difficult situations?

SESSION FIVE

The first Passover

As we left the Israelites at the end of the last study they were about to prepare for the first Passover. This event is so important in the Old Testament religion that several ancient writers wrote about it. Our Bible contains several accounts each highlighting a different significance in the events. The following passage is one description of how the final disaster happened. It is also an explanation of the meaning of the festival.

[21] Moses called for all the leaders of Israel and said to them, "Each of you is to choose a lamb or a young goat and kill it, so that your families can celebrate Passover. [22] Take a sprig of hyssop, dip it in the bowl containing the animal's blood, and wipe the blood on the door-posts and the beam above the door of your house. Not one of you is to leave the house until morning. [23] When the LORD goes through Egypt to kill the Egyptians, he will see the blood on the beams and the door-posts and will not let the Angel of Death enter your houses and kill you. [24] You and your children must obey these rules for ever. [25] When you enter the land that the LORD has promised to give you, you must perform this ritual. [26] When your children ask you, 'What does this ritual mean?' [27] you will answer, 'It is the sacrifice of Passover to honour the LORD, because he passed over the houses of the Israelites in Egypt. He killed the Egyptians, but spared us.'"

The Israelites knelt down and worshipped. [28] Then they went and did what the LORD had commanded Moses and Aaron.

[31] That same night the king sent for Moses and Aaron and said, "Get out, you and your Israelites! Leave my country; go and worship the LORD, as you asked. [32] Take your sheep, goats, and cattle, and leave. Also pray for a blessing on me."

[33] The Egyptians urged the people to hurry and leave the country; they said, "We will all be dead if you don't leave." [34] So the people filled their baking-pans with unleavened dough, wrapped them in clothing, and carried them on their shoulders.
Exodus 12.21-28, 31-34

To talk about

- Below is a list of festivals that are kept today.
  - Christmas day
  - Remembrance Sunday
  - Easter
  - Harvest festival
  - Bonfire night
  - Mothering Sunday
  - New Year's Day
- Talk with other members of the group about why we celebrate each of these festivals in the way we do.
- Not all of these festivals are based on historical events. Does this matter?
- In some countries there are special holidays to commemorate military campaigns and victories. Are some historical events better forgotten?

Dedication

In the account of the escape from Egypt, two other Jewish customs are explained. The first is the dedication of the first-born male:

[1] The LORD said to Moses, [2] "Dedicate all the first-born males to me, for every first-born male Israelite and every first-born male animal belongs to me."
Exodus 13.1-2

In the ancient world first-born children were
sometimes killed as a sacrifice to pagan gods. Their
bodies were put in the foundations of ancient
buildings, supposedly to give the building strength.
Here the writer shows that God wants the first-born
to be dedicated to him (not killed), and that the
practice of dedication stems from something that
actually happened in history.

• Can you think of any ways in which we dedicate
  children today? Why do we do it?

The Festival of Unleavened Bread

The Jewish Festival of Unleavened Bread probably
has its origins in a ceremony held in the spring to
celebrate the barley harvest. Since it was held just
before the Passover, both festivals came to be
associated with the escape from Egypt. (Unleavened
bread is made without yeast - the bread does not rise,
so it is flat and hard.)

In the studies so far we have seen how the Israelites
began to trust God. Now they start their journey to
the land which God had promised them.

• Imagine you are a newspaper photographer. You
  have been allowed space for three photographs to
  tell the story of Moses' life so far. What would they
  be? Compare your choice with the rest of the group.

New Testament Link

Read Luke 22.14-20 . . .

> ¹⁴ When the hour came, Jesus took his place at the
> table with the apostles. ¹⁵ He said to them, "I have
> wanted so much to eat this Passover meal with you

before I suffer! [16] For I tell you, I will never eat it until it is given its full meaning in the Kingdom of God."

[17] Then Jesus took a cup, gave thanks to God, and said, "Take this and share it among yourselves. [18] I tell you that from now on I will not drink this wine until the Kingdom of God comes."

[19] Then he took a piece of bread, gave thanks to God, broke it, and gave it to them, saying, "This is my body, which is given for you. Do this in memory of me." [20] In the same way, he gave them the cup after the supper, saying, "This cup is God's new covenant sealed with my blood, which is poured out for you."

It was at Passover time that Jesus was crucified. To the early Christians, it seemed that Jesus himself had taken the place of the lambs which were sacrificed. St Paul writes: "For our Passover Festival is ready, now that Christ, our Passover lamb, has been sacrificed." (1 Corinthians 5.7) Our celebration of Easter has traditionally been linked with the Jewish Passover.

- Which Christian festival or celebration means the most to you:
  - Christmas?
  - Pentecost?
  - Easter?
  - Ascension?
- Explain to the group why it is special.

SESSION SIX

The great escape

Now the people of Israel have escaped. Imagine the headlines in the Egyptian papers next morning! Look at these possible headlines. What might the first few lines of each story say?

- CRUEL EPIDEMIC STRIKES
- MYSTERY BUG CHAOS LETS SLAVES ESCAPE
- "SLAVES BROUGHT DISEASE," SAYS KING

Each of these stories and the account in Exodus reflect the different points of view of the writers.

[5] When the king of Egypt was told that the people had escaped, he and his officials changed their minds and said, "What have we done? We have let the Israelites escape, and we have lost them as our slaves!" [6] The king got his war chariot and his army ready. [7] He set out with all his chariots, including the six hundred finest, commanded by their officers. [8] The LORD made the king stubborn, and he pursued the Israelites, who were leaving triumphantly. [9] The Egyptian army, with all the horses, chariots, and drivers, pursued them and caught up with them where they were camped by the Red Sea near Pi Hahiroth and Baal Zephon.

[10] When the Israelites saw the king and his army marching against them, they were terrified and cried out to the LORD for help. [11] They said to Moses, "Weren't there any graves in Egypt? Did you have to bring us out here in the desert to die? Look what you have done by bringing us out of Egypt! [12] Didn't we tell you before we left that this would happen? We told you to leave us alone and let us go on being slaves of

the Egyptians. It would be better to be slaves there than to die here in the desert." *Exodus 14.5-12*

Moses reassures the people that God will save them, and God continues to tell Moses what to do. So . . .

[21] Moses held out his hand over the sea, and the LORD drove the sea back with a strong east wind. It blew all night and turned the sea into dry land. The water was divided, [22] and the Israelites went through the sea on dry ground, with walls of water on both sides. [23] The Egyptians pursued them and went after them into the sea with all their horses, chariots, and drivers. [24] Just before dawn the LORD looked down from the pillar of fire and cloud at the Egyptian army and threw them into panic. [25] He made the wheels of their chariots get stuck, so that they moved with great difficulty. The Egyptians said, "The LORD is fighting for the Israelites against us. Let's get out of here!"

[26] The LORD said to Moses, "Hold out your hand over the sea, and the water will come back over the Egyptians and their chariots and drivers." [27] So Moses held out his hand over the sea, and at daybreak the water returned to its normal level. The Egyptians tried to escape from the water, but the LORD threw them into the sea. [28] The water returned and covered the chariots, the drivers, and all the Egyptian army that had followed the Israelites into the sea; not one of them was left. [29] But the Israelites walked through the sea on dry ground, with walls of water on both sides.

[30] On that day the LORD saved the people of Israel from the Egyptians, and the Israelites saw them lying dead on the seashore. [31] When the Israelites saw the great power with which the LORD had defeated the Egyptians, they stood in awe of the LORD; and they had faith in the LORD and in his servant Moses. *Exodus 14.21-31*

We're thirsty!

Although the Israelites are now out of Egypt, life is far from easy for them. Problems begin to arise, and before they have gone far there is a minor crisis:

> ¹ The whole Israelite community left the desert of Sin, moving from one place to another at the command of the LORD. They made camp at Rephidim, but there was no water there to drink. ² They complained to Moses and said, "Give us water to drink."
>
> Moses answered, "Why are you complaining? Why are you putting the LORD to the test?"
>
> ³ But the people were very thirsty and continued to complain to Moses. They said, "Why did you bring us our of Egypt? To kill us and our children and our livestock with thirst?"
>
> ⁴ Moses prayed earnestly to the LORD and said, "What can I do with these people? They are almost ready to stone me."
>
> ⁵ The LORD said to Moses, "Take some of the leaders of Israel with you, and go on ahead of the people. Take along the stick with which you struck the Nile. ⁶ I will stand before you on a rock at Mount Sinai. Strike the rock, and water will come out of it for the people to drink." Moses did so in the presence of the leaders of Israel.   *Exodus 17.1-6*

- In this kind of situation what does Moses do:
  - side with the Israelites?
  - side with God?
  - act as a go-between, not giving particular support to either side?

Moses must be as hungry and thirsty as the rest of them. He must also know that as leader he is a prime target if the Israelites are attacked. He must miss the safety he has left behind too.

- Look at your answer to the last question again. What does this tell you about Moses? Which of these words best describes him: loyal, scared, faithful, obedient, gullible, trusting? Compare your answers with the others in the group.

To talk about

Although the Israelites have been slaves in Egypt, some of them prefer the security of being there to the uncertainty of following Moses and trusting God.

- Can you think of someone else who has given up everything to go where God sent them? If you had two words to describe them what would they be?

For many years a close relationship has existed between God and members of the family of Israel. They are gradually coming to know more about him.

- What do you think the Israelites have learned about God so far? Which of these words do you think they might use to describe God: warrior, advisor, defender, magician, policeman, healer, provider? See if the other group members have chosen the same as you. Be prepared to defend your choice.

New Testament link

In 1 Corinthians 10.11, Paul looks back at the events we have studied, and says of them "these things were written down as a warning for us".

- Do you agree?
- What do you think we can learn from the Exodus story?

BRITISH AND FOREIGN BIBLE SOCIETY
Stonehill Green, Westlea, SWINDON   SN5 7DG, England
© Bible Society 1992
ISBN 0564-08025X

Unless otherwise stated, quotations from the Bible are from the Good News Bible,
published by the Bible Societies/Haper Collins © American Bible Society, New York,
1966, 1971 and 4th edition 1976.

A catalogue record for this book is available from the British Library
Printed and bound in Great Britain by Stanley L Hunt
Cover design by Paul Thomas
Bible Societies exist to provide resources for Bible distribution and use. The British
and Foreign Bible Society (BFBS) is a member of the United Bible Societies, an
international partnership working in over 180 countries. Their common aim is to
reach all people with the Bible, or some part of it, in a language they can understand
and a price they can afford. Parts of the Bible have now been translated into over
1900 languages. Bible Societies aim to help every church at every point where it
uses the Bible. You are invited to share in this work by your prayers and gifts.
Bible Society in your county will be very happy to provide details of its activity.